Marshmallow
Ice cream

Nazmin Akthar

BookLeaf Publishing

Presentation by *BookLeaf Publishing*

Web: www.bookleafpub.com

E-mail: info@bookleafpub.com

ISBN: 9789358313857

First edition 2025

DEDICATION

To my daughter Amyra,

my best friend,

my biggest inspiration and support,

and the brain behind the name, *Marshmallow Ice cream.*

I love you.

PREFACE

For as long as I remember, I have always loved to write. Poems, short stories, opinion pieces, articles; absolutely anything. I have always found the process of writing very healing, even if the only person who would read the end product was me.

Unfortunately, the dreaded writer's block then appeared in my life, and it has taken a very long time to shake it off. I guess you could say that these poems are a post-recovery collection.

The themes and messages of each of my poems are those which I care deeply about and which I think we as a society need to discuss and address to effect long-term and sustainable changes. Some of these themes and messages will be very obvious; perhaps you will find the poems bland even. Others may appear cryptic, and you may come to a conclusion about the subject matter that is different from what I envisaged. But that is exactly how real life is, right?

Whatever you take away from it all, I hope it is positive. Thank you for your support. I hope I do not disappoint.

Alif

There were times I thought I had lost all favour,
thought I had reached the end,
thought the present was my forever future,
but on each occasion,
right as I reached the last station,
an invisible force appeared to guide me further.

Even when I made mistakes,
even when I should have known better,
and wondered which error of mine had led to
this punishment,
mercy was bestowed,
I was given breaks,
one after the other.

Could there be a greater blessing than never
being alone?
A permanent guide, sharing lessons but always
with love and mercy, without fetter.
Sometimes you need to feel the pain, the fear,

to appreciate the moments when you breathe
without either,
but only ever as much as you can bear,
and never the bearer of the burden of another.

Starlight

A traveller's guide, nature's map.
Freely available to all, whether rich or poor,
of course, whether you can use or appreciate the
light of the star,
is definitely dependent on circumstance.
Encrypted messages written all across the sky,
open to all, yet only for some to decipher.
Indiscriminate,
fair,
a witness of all actions, no one can hide.

Tiny diamonds illuminating your way,
following wherever you go,
silent but reassuring.

Small but mighty also.
Remember, the sun is also a star,
and I don't think the septillion are any less
impressive.

My daughter

It looks like I am holding her hand,
because I am the adult,
and she is so small.
Truth is, we are equals holding one another.

Her fist is smaller than my index finger,
but with her tiny hands, she gives me support,
she reassures me that she believes in me,
encourages me to carry on.

She stands with me; she walks with me.
She doesn't know how long the journey is or the
destination,
but she still takes the next step, matching my
pace, my stride.

A beautiful little girl,
full of innocence and a little mischievousness,

permeating confidence,
already radiating with a sense of justice,
understanding right from wrong.

My daughter, my saviour.
She doesn't know it, but that is what she is.

The Princess

A smart princess, strong and logical.
Methods she possesses are not understood by all,
making her seem difficult, hard work.
Yes, she needs time and patience, but what is
wrong with that when the end result is bullseye?
Rightfully the leader,
a queen in the making, with the right tools if
they are given to her.

An empathetic princess, kind and supportive,
merciful to those who deserve it, ignoring those
who use no chance to be better.
Yield she does not when she knows she is
standing for what is equitable and proper.
Resilient, even if a little nervous, she just needs
a little cheer,
and a lot less of the comparing and the unhealthy
competition.

A loyal princess, fair and transparent,
maybe her honesty is not everyone's cup of tea,
despite it allegedly being the quality we all hold
dear.
Young, yet so deeply wise,

resourceful when she sets her mind to a task, age is after all a mere number.

Marshmallow Ice cream

Hello, my name is Marshmallow.
And, my name is Ice cream.
Together we are Marshmallow Ice cream.

We have similarities and differences,
our individual and collective origins from all
over the world.
China, Italy, Egypt, to name a few,
a combination of that which was sourced from
the wild and the other so readily available.

One of us performs best in the heat, the other
rules in the cold,
yet somehow, together we work, very well,
bringing flavour,
a moment of relaxation.

We can perform individually perfectly well, and
we do,
but we are also a great team together.
A squishy, loving hug,
just what the doctor ordered.

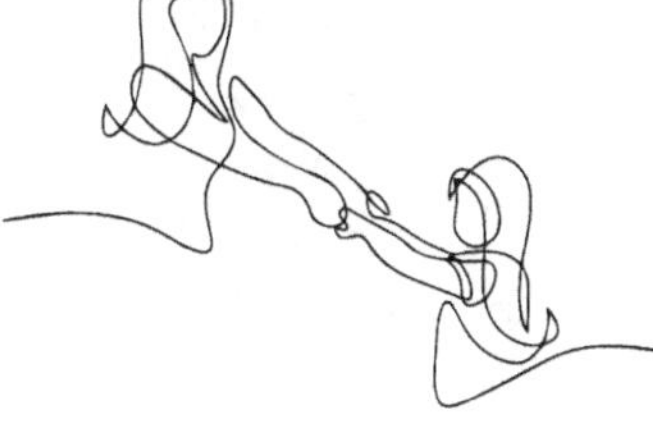

The worst pear tree

The worst pear tree.
Deformed fruits that taste awful,
the juice disgusting more so.
What is the point of existing if you are neither
good looking nor useful?

Axe it, uproot it.
Waste of space; remove it.
Is it the soil that caused it to be so bizarre?
Or is this just a freak of nature?
Maybe another tree will fare better here,
certainly better than this one did.

If only they had taken the time to learn and
understand,
if only they had thought outside the box,
if only they had not made a judgement based on
their limited knowledge.
If only they weren't so hasty,
they wouldn't have destroyed the best quince
tree.

Fruit bowl

A clear bowl,
with little spiral engravings as a pattern,
to set it apart,
sturdy, even though it is made of glass.

Pick and choose which fruit you place within it,
a particular type,
or one of each,
few of this, a bit more of that.

So long as they don't expire,
and become a total waste,
it doesn't matter with which you decorate,
actually no, with which you sustain.

And if they do go out of date,
straight to the compost heap it goes,
or even the bin if that's the safest option.
Removing toxicity – that is the main aim.

It also doesn't matter if sometimes the fruit bowl
is filled with chocolate instead,
or sweets or other sugary treats.
It also wouldn't matter if for a little while you
didn't use the fruit bowl at all.
If that is what you want and you are not harming
yourself,

why would the fruit bowl mind?

How is your fruit bowl looking today?
Do you have what you really want in it, or is it
time for a change?

The view from the train

The reflection in the train window is mine,
yet somehow it looks different,
a little more polished than usual,
is that the effect of the vehicle or the journey?

The passenger sees so much,
even if for a fleeting moment,
does a station itself not say a little something,
about a city, a country, a village?
Some knowledge is better than none.

The reflection can change so easily too,
a new light, different weather,
a change in scenery,
even a simple clean,
and you will find another picture.

And therein lies the difference,
the train window will let you see,
not guarantee that you will learn.
Some knowledge is better than none,
but it is not a good basis for decisions.

Taplow

A village with history,
a parish of quirks.
Elizabethan but touched by Buddhism too,
an endearing little court.

Touched by the four elements,
the Thames, the Jubilee,
the Quarry,
the hill fort reaching the sky,
the gas holder site providing fuel for fire.
What has this place not seen?

A mixture of occupations,
hotels and boats, paper making, corn and cotton,
and the battleground also,
for employment rights that is.

Now a place for shelter, walls that aim to keep
you safe,
a new development of homes, a new community,
open spaces for fresh air too.
These are, of course, the most important needs
of the hour,
a place to live,
a residence of well-being and comfort.
A place for new events, new memories,

and some histories that even the air of Taplow
does not know about,
cherished.

Rooftop Woes

I don't like it hot,
I don't like it cold.
Not too sunny, not too windy,
definitely not rainy.
But nothing is ever just right,
certainly not on the rooftop.

The best friend

17

Hot water bottle
An alternate medicine
Careful, do not burst

A cup of tea

Put the kettle on,
a nice cup of tea always makes things better,
a cure for tiredness,
say goodbye to sleep.

Stir the tea bag for at least three minutes,
let the flavours release,
that will get rid of the migraine,
and the stomach pain,
and will deal with your sugar levels too.

Careful, don't spill the tea.
You will have to change the plasters covering
your chapped hands,
and you know going up the stairs to find more
will make you feel faint again.

Oh, the tea is quite cold. Is the kettle broken? Or
the stove?
Best go check and call for help if necessary.
It's important to get the right diagnostics,
and the correct assistance in good time.
Isn't it?

Isn't it?

Winter

I love all seasons, but I love the winter the most.
I love the snow,
it makes everything so beautiful,
hiding all the imperfections,
enveloping all into a festive embrace.

My constant friend,
my only friend,
giving me something to do with its arrival,
making me the same as everyone else again.

Don't get me wrong,
I have nothing against the summer and enjoy it
too.
But the social expectations that come with it,
always increase my stress and anxiety,
you know.

You see, everyone is there for you,
until they realise that they have to be
permanently there,
for you.
It is not like a fractured leg.
The depression, the learning difficulties,
they are all here to stay.

The snow covers me,
so I don't seem so different,
it protects me,
it lets me be,
on the days that I am not as coherent.

In the driving seat

A recurring dream,
driving without shoes.
A dangerous sign,
illegal too.

In the driving seat,
responsible for all the passengers,
and everyone else on the road,
appropriate footwear,
is an absolute must.

So many stops to make,
errands to run,
passengers to pick up and drop off.
Decisions to make about each turning,
each road.
Permanently, again and again.

Sometimes I forget a task even though I
remembered it just moments before.
I know that is terrible.
It is never on purpose,
there is just so much to remember,
checking for speed bumps,
keeping my eyes peeled for pedestrians,
seatbelts, petrol, engine oil,

is the MOT due soon?
But never would I forget my shoes, no.

I hate letting anyone down,
I cannot slow down either,
there is just no time.
Constantly changing gears and lanes,
until I can finally take a break,
and then I have to start all over again.

In the driving seat,
the dream is a warning,
rest,
before you forget to put anything on your feet.

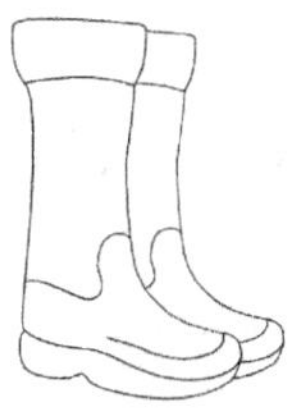

Lost in love

Lost in love,
a tragic tale.
A story that is priceless,
yet up for sale.

A charming prince he was,
her life companion.
Without the royal carriage for he needed none.
He ruled hearts and moulded minds,
with goodness, sincerity and sense.

Listen, moon, today is Sunday.
The prince is now hurt, struck by malady,
resembling a stone,
dense.
Is that because of you, or without you?

Quietly, secretly, the obstacles of life start to
appear.
Misunderstandings, some due to external forces,
some thanks to mood swings.
Cousins, greedy siblings, villains in all
disguises.
Fairyland isn't far though,
nor is the end of the time.
Can true love be found again, or is it lost
forever?

Change is constant but not always inevitable,
like a thorn accompanying a rose,
she is trying to save the world but getting
betrayed by the vultures around it,
a chance of happiness snatched away from her
clutches,
at the eleventh hour,
thunder and lightning accompanying the event,
because the truth they already know.

Ok calm down,
it is just a TV show.

Apologies for the delay

I am tired; I want to go to sleep.
Alas, I have deadlines to keep.
My neck is starting to burn up,
oh no, another panic attack.
No seriously, what a terrible bodily response,
to make you freeze at that exact moment that
you should be speeding up.

Maybe a short nap?
A really short one. Oh, but what if I do that thing
again where I don't wake up from the nap for
another three hours?
I really don't like that; I end up feeling worse
and even less productive.
But I really am tired,
the power station is shutting down.

I should prepare a to-do list,
you know,
to keep on track.
But I won't lie; there is no denying,
sometimes, all the list does is tell me I need
magical powers.

How about if I wake up early? That would give
me a head start.
Of course, to do that, I need to give up my love
for the snooze game.
4.45 am is a good time to start the day. Oh, it's 5
am now?
Maybe fifteen more minutes, maybe another ten.
If I start at 6 am, that will still be two hours
before I need to set off.
If I start at 6.30 am, that is still a whole 90
minutes?
Oh, look at that. I am officially on the clock
now.
Why do I do that? Now I am still behind but also
exhausted from not having properly slept, rested.

Inevitably, it will lead to the same end,
an email that starts with 'apologies for the delay',
words that I should have engraved onto my
gravestone.

What is the saying about those who do the same
thing again and again expecting a different
result?

Fool's gold

Once upon a time, there was a boss,
a manager if you will.
Incompetent and clumsy, yet full of self-praise,
living in the past, forgetting they need to
function in the present.
Blaming everyone else for their failings,
when a simple apology would have sufficed.
Instead of cementing the team,
playing colleagues against each other.
Pretending to be a friend whilst criticising all in
the same breath,
thinking the world revolves around them,
with their impossible deadlines and last-minute
demands.
Perhaps because they know the game will be
over,
as soon as the box is opened,
so everything needs to be done to keep the lid
firmly shut.

Without prejudice

She shouldn't have married someone from a
different culture, different ethnicity.
I didn't; he still gave me a black eye.
She shouldn't have married outside of her faith.
I didn't; he still burnt me with a scalding hot
iron.

She was too focused on her career and didn't
give him enough time.
I didn't work; he still broke my arm.
Can you blame him for lashing out when he had
to take on the responsibility of a financially
dependent adult? He was under so much
pressure.
When I did work, he punched my face then too.

She should have let her parents choose.
I did. He later refused to let me speak to them,
even when they were seriously unwell.
Well, she must have done something to
aggravate him,
raised her voice,
dressed inappropriately,
didn't listen to a demand? All demands are of
course reasonable.

I didn't, yet I am still dead.

Fenced

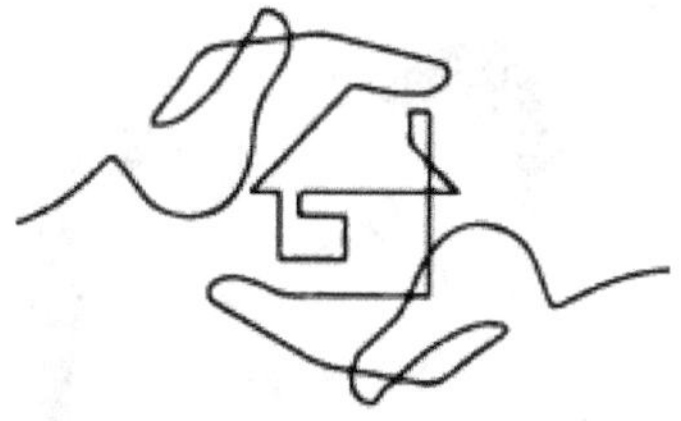

Why are you raising the height of your picket
fence?
It's so big you can no longer see beyond it?
Who are you trying to hide from?
What have you done to need to take this step?

A little boy was brutally murdered.
6 years old.
My daughter's age.
At a time when he should be learning his
phonics,
his dead body is lying cold.

You tell me that if I have nothing to hide, then a
little stopping and searching,
questioning and investigating,
a little bit of suspicion will not hurt.
It is all for the greater good.
You tell me that I will be fine,
so long as I am on the right side.

Answer me this,
what did that little child do to deserve to be
stabbed 27 times?
What could any child ever do to deserve such
brutality, such callousness?
You call it an exception,
a rare occurrence,
it won't happen to me,
I am one of the good ones.
Yet an innocent child exists no more,
because someone decided they deserved to die,
that it was the right thing to do,
for this angel to say his eternal goodbye.
What chance then do I have?

The picket fence needs to be higher,
for me and my loved ones to stay safe.
If you cannot understand that,
then perhaps,
perhaps I need to be safe from you.

Sui Generis

You know what is truly of its own kind?
Really unique in this world of abuse and
misinformation?
The one who still retains balance,
even at the risk of ostracisation.

Proportionality,
fair, just and reasonable,
words scrawled across law books,
in all realms and sovereignties.
Yet the one who actually asks for these
principles to be applied,
is written off as the crook.

What is the worst thing you can be?
That which you hate.
It really is peculiar how many people understand
this too late,
and some just never do.

From an eye for an eye makes the whole world
blind, to bulldozing down an entire residential
building for the actions of an unknown one.
From promoting democracy, law and order,
to deciding that anyone can be their own judge,
jury and executioner.

There really is nothing like it,
when you can still feel the injustice of punishing
the innocent,
whilst the guilty walk free,
when you can distinguish between right and
wrong,
every day, this is becoming rarer to find.

Chandrabindu

A culture so ancient,
yet a country so young,
partitioned at least twice,
communities in existence for centuries,
but nevertheless born new.

The respected land,
the wounds from war still so fresh,
the blood that was spilled,
still gleaming on the flag.

The luscious greenery,
the red sun rising,
saluting the queens of the golden land,
the Birangona.

Rivers call on more rivers,
Padma, Meghna, Surma,
Brahmaputra,
meandering through sites of paddy fields,
succulent tea gardens,
harvests of pumpkins and bottle gourds.
The fish dance around in their beautiful sarees,
the majestic animals at Sunderbans walk with
their heads held high.

On one side we have Hazrat Shah Jalal's Dargah,
on the other, Sompur Mahavihara,
and amongst them all, Lalbagh Fort.

The shining land,
adapting itself,
changing with time,
but keeping its essence intact.
Just like chandrabindu,
that modifies pronunciation,
activating the other vocals,
those which others may not have,
perhaps may not even hear.

Chandrabindu.
A supporting act to the alphabet,
but its importance is by no means less.

Dhaka Muslin

The royal threads,
once a status symbol,
adorning the Mughal sovereigns,
and statues of goddesses of ancient Greece.

Now as dead as a dodo,
killed by corporate greed,
using allegations of immorality.
Do I call it the perfect example of how cruel
commercialisation can be,
or evidence of how easily puritanism can be
used to destroy heritage?

I hear there are calls for its resurrection,
I hope they succeed.

But it does make me wonder,
when is it right to seek a revival of the past,
and when is it best to leave something in the
pages of history?

Acknowledgement is always essential,
but are there times when this is sufficient,
along with an acceptance that times have
changed?

A tightrope of a question.

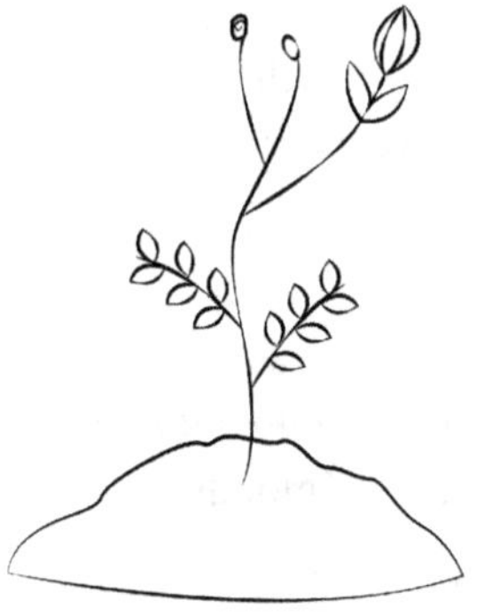

Art class

I drew a painting at school,
I was about 12 years old then.

It was of a cat,
laying eggs in a nest up a tree,
houses replaced the clouds in the sky.

I can't remember which artist we were learning
about,
I think the theme was about using symbolism.
Either way, it wasn't a very good piece,
and I realised very quickly that art was not my
forte.

However, now I think younger me was onto
something.
As I look around and see empty skyscrapers,
unreachable to the homeless,
being taken care of by those who cannot afford
to pay their own rent.

Maybe the point of art class isn't about being
good.
Maybe it is about a messy canvas,
helping you to cleanse your vision.

Inheritance

Always together, segregated, you say.
They don't integrate, work hard, you say.
They just don't fit in.

They smell, look at their clothes.
Such unhealthy food, immoral practices, you
say.
Jobless, lazy, messy.
Others managed to come with nothing and
succeed,
why couldn't they?

It's all excuses, you say.
Attacking your culture,
disrespecting the opportunities you say you
gave.

You are the flag-bearer of your so-called
heritage,
they are erasing it, you say.

But when will you say,
acknowledge and accept,
all that you complain of,
is due to the trauma you caused,
passed down from generation to generation,

which continues to be their inheritance,
that will pass onto generations some more?

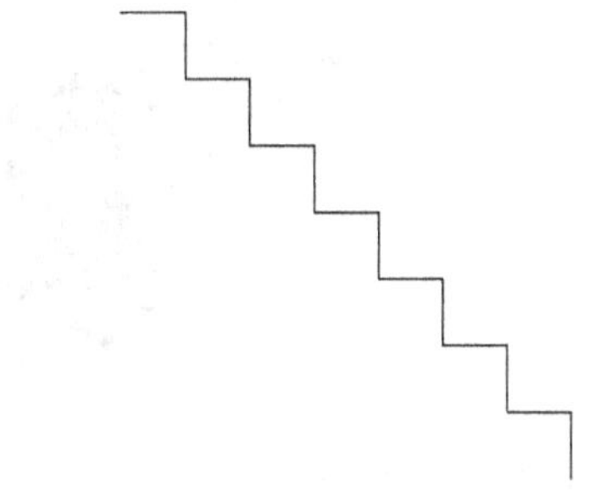

School's out

How is it that with more knowledge,
we have become less wise?

We know we are all different,
that everyone has their own strengths and
weaknesses,
different needs and different desires,
yet children are still measured in the exact same
way?

It is easy to teach someone who already knows
how to learn.
True talent is being able to help those who are
not quite there yet,
struggling,
unsure,
unsafe.

Be the teacher,
indiscriminately,
then watch them blossom to the same levels of
greatness,
but in different ways,
that would be your real trophy.

Vegetable Biryani

An interminable argument,
soon to be a villain original story,
without a doubt, a debate just that strong.

An obsession with the ingredients,
ignorance of the methodology.
It's pilau, it's pilau!

So what if one is focused on a method of
draining and layering,
and the other on absorption and mixing?
It cannot be biryani without meat!
Meat takes longer to be consumption-ready,
the biryani process cannot be replicated with the
invading vegetables.

So what if biryani can be made with prawns too,
and eggs?
So what if eggs can be cooked as quickly as
vegetables?
So what if pieces of lamb have always been
layered with potatoes in biryani recipes?

It cannot be biryani unless there is meat
involved.

It will be called pilau regardless of how it has
been prepared.

So what if every other dish has been, and can be,
adapted to be inclusive of dietary requirements?
So what if we can see variations of the same
dishes across countries, all adding an ethnic
twist to make it their own?

No, no, computer does not comprehend.

But I will not be stopped.
I see you.

Long live vegetable biryani.

Not in my name

Once upon a time,
I held a very naïve belief,
quite embarrassing, really.

Sick of being othered,
I thought,
if only someone like me was in charge.

That's the issue with wishes, though,
you need to be very clear, very specific,
otherwise, you will be caught out by the
loopholes,
as I have been.

You see, when I said someone like me,
I didn't mean the superficial similarities,
but rather the shared beliefs and experiences.
Even then, I was not looking for my clone,
just some understanding,
to make me feel like I belong.

Unfortunately, cosmetic similarities are all that
is on the menu,
and I am being told it is a moment to celebrate,
to be proud.

No. I will not applaud,
certainly not for someone who would be ready
to tie my hands,
and throw me away,
into a cold, dark pit.

Looking like me isn't enough.
I will not support you,
your atrocities will not happen in my name.

Foreigner

How do you pronounce 'swede'?
Does it rhyme with feed or fed?
Deed or dread?

Do I pronounce the 'r' in Ochre? The 'h' in
Durham?

Why do we ignore the middle sound in
Worcester? And Gloucester?

For I have never heard any of these words
spoken before,
I have only ever read them.

The house is on fire

When in trouble, do not shout for help.
Shout 'fire, fire'!
Do not tell them a little girl has been kidnapped.
Tell them you are looking for a little dog
forcibly taken,
or that a cow has been hit by a runaway driver.

Do not tell them you were beaten,
pushed down the stairs and left to die.
Tell them, you are a witness to tax fraud.

When in trouble, do not shout for help.
Shout something that will matter to those
listening.
You being stabbed to death will not affect them
personally,
the curtains may twitch, but the door shall not
open.

But the phantom fire in your house?
That could spread you see,
and so a phone call might just be made.

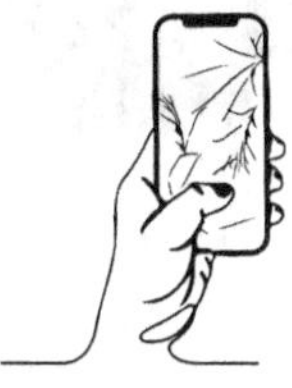

Clueless

When I finally spoke up,
they all cried.
I left.
I felt like the problem,
there was no turning back from what had
happened,
or to be more precise, what did not happen.

They continue to wonder why no one stays,
or why there is so much unhappiness for those
who remain.

And the cycle shall continue.

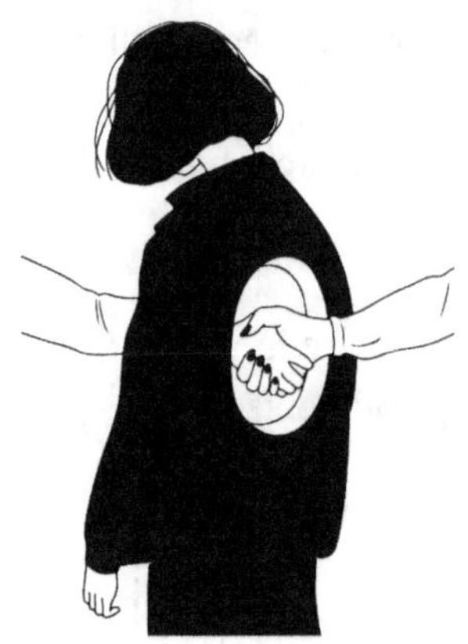

Crutches

A profession focused on good,
and good is all you shall hear.
You will not hear the rest.
After all, how can you complain about that
which is focused on good?

Do put your health first,
your well-being, and your family.
Of course, we are supportive of a work-life
balance.
But not before completing our work,
even if that appears out of nowhere,
all of a sudden one evening.
For good reason, of course,
competition is tough,
we need to stay ahead,
that is the only way to carry on doing good.

Look after yourself.
Take a day off and don't take any calls,
or log on to check emails.
Except ours.
That has to be the priority.
No, it is not toxic for us to say that.
We are working for the greater good, after all.

You won't be paid your worth,
there just is not enough money.
Promotion opportunities are also limited,
but admittedly, learning and development is a
constant.

A profession of good purpose,
of that, there is no doubt,
but not void of toxicity.
Most at risk of burnout,
majority here to stay, the only place they can be,
because the grass is not greener elsewhere.
The grass is even more poisonous, in fact.

The fourth emergency service,
genuinely a place of good,
but in complete crisis,
because even its crutches are plastered,
and these broken crutches are being taken away.

Mothering

How do you manage all this?
Oh, just somehow.

Wake up early, long before dawn even decides to
stir,
iron the clothes,
fold away those that are dry,
put away toys, games, books,
everything from the day before.

Gather the cups of unfinished tea from every
room,
wash these and make another cup,
maybe even coffee this time,
it is going to be a long day, like it always is.

Start to make breakfast,
packed lunch,
prepare for your own lunch.

Where is the to-do list pad?
Prepare the list for the new day,
carry over from the day before.
Must remember to pay that car parking fine,
and check those meter readings too.

School run time,
rush back for the first meeting,
and the next,
checking in with seniors,
supervising the juniors,
completing other projects of the day.

School run time again,
a break to make a post-school snack,
check the homework set for the day.
Back to work, fitting in some charity work too,
advocating for others,
helping those in need,
helping the business too,
looking for ways to bring in more work,
oh, almost forgot to order a wedding gift,
there is a baby shower to plan too.

Time for homework,
some play time, an activity or two,
time for a tablet for the headache too,
get clothes ready for a networking event,
while scribbling notes for an upcoming
presentation.

Some more work, urgent deadline has appeared,
need to add purchasing concealer on the list.

It is midnight, but the work for the day isn't
done.
Wash the dishes,
online shopping,
check the social messages,
share a social media post,
while cuddling with a hot water bottle.

How do you manage all this?
Oh, just somehow.

Please, I need to see a doctor

Please, I need to see a doctor.
Something feels wrong.
I am starting to feel pain,
and a lot of tiredness.

No, I am not struggling to breathe.
Yes, I can move my arms and legs.
But it is starting to hurt.

Pharmacy? That is an option.
They gave me some vitamins,
some pain medication.

Please, I need to see a doctor.
I am getting weaker,
more and more tired.
The pain is starting to spread,
and I can see a rash and some bruising.

Telephone consultation?
Ok, if that is all that is available.
Yes, I guess it could be stress related,
but the rash is getting worse and I cannot sleep
at night.
It is starting to affect work.

Please, I need to see a doctor.
I fainted today.
The pain is now unbearable,
and I have been vomiting too.
It has been four hours since I was brought into
A&E,
how much longer?

More blood tests? I understand.
Please let me know when to attend so I can book
time off.
No, I do not need a sick note; I cannot afford to
take leave.
When will I receive the results?

Please, I need to see a doctor.
I have a question.
Had I been assessed properly from the
beginning,
could this surgery have been avoided?

De-choiced

I went to vote today.
The choice was between a box jellyfish and a
mosquito.
I thought to myself,
a box jellyfish is known to be venomous,
whilst the mosquito is small,
only dangerous when it carries a disease.
I chose the mosquito.
I thought, they are irritating, but the harm will be
less.
Choosing the lesser of two evils,
limiting the damage.
I was wrong.
I did not have all the information.
The mosquito had bitten a deadly snake,
and was now freely spreading the poison,
at a much faster rate than the box jellyfish could
ever have managed.

Boxed

Invisible helmets covering our minds,
stopping knowledge from seeping in.
Sunglasses obscuring our vision,
preventing light from penetrating within.

In a bubble, boxed in,
unable to see or hear,
unable to understand, even less able to respect,
despite being in the free and open.

Self-righteousness fuelling prejudice,
refusing to appreciate,
it is possible to co-exist,
without having to compromise your sense of
self.

Pointing fingers,
adding spices where not needed,
not realising that there is a parallel story,
with someone else pointing fingers,
adding oil.

The worst of the seven deadly sins is most
certainly pride.
If only you could think outside the box,
see the full picture,

that a lot of what you use as evidence,
has most likely been said and done under peer
pressure.
For there is someone just like you on the other
side,
intolerant, full of ego.
It is not safe to share their true thoughts,
for fear of reprisals,
especially when they know they face equal
danger from you.

If only you would realise,
you are only hating yourself,
when you hate the other.

Accomplice

The accomplice,
the wretched leech,
the one who knows the difference between right
and wrong,
but still throws petrol on the already burning
logs,
for profit.

Talentless flop.

Centre of the universe

Tiny seedlings,
our future trees,
their growth,
key to the world's survival.

Little sponges,
with exploring minds,
the architects of tomorrow,
dependent on their today.

They are the centre of the universe,
in need of support, sustenance,
encouragement, love,
hope.

Anyone who prioritises themselves over our
plants,
does not deserve to be involved in their growth,
or reap any of the rewards.

My oak tree

Provider of shade,
lateral support,
strong, sturdy, reliable.

Resilient no matter the day, the season,
a reminder that our strength comes from within,
an inspiration to all that can comprehend.

Existing since time immemorial,
yet still keeping pace with the era,
at peace with the journey,
encouraging others to find their place too.

A timeless friendship,
my oak tree,
my best friend.

Veranda stories

Hop, hop again.
Jump and tag,
running around the pickle jars.

Mango pickle,
tamarind, gooseberry,
soaking in the sun to settle and enhance their
taste,
even naga pickle,
that one is not for the faint hearted.

Poppadoms drying on one side,
shutki fish drying on the other,
everyone on guard lest the crows appear to steal,
smell strong enough to make everyone else run
away.

Playing Ful Gutti,
not very well admittedly,

listening to tales of ancestors going far back,
all amidst the hustle and bustle of the veranda.

For the first, and last time.
It will be time for the flight soon,
and soon after that,
it will be time to divide up the veranda,
and settle all claims and stakes in it.

Ignore the door bell

Shut the door,
ignore the door bell,
don't let anyone in.
One thing or other will happen,
it will become messy again.
I am tired of cleaning,
I barely have time for it,
so when I do manage to tidy up the house,
I would much rather maintain it.
I know I have a dishwasher,
and a washing machine,
but loading and unloading takes time,
and if I forget about the laundry, it will smell
too.
I cannot explain it,
I need to do it myself,
having to reject offers of help will just make it
even more awkward,
so just shut the door.

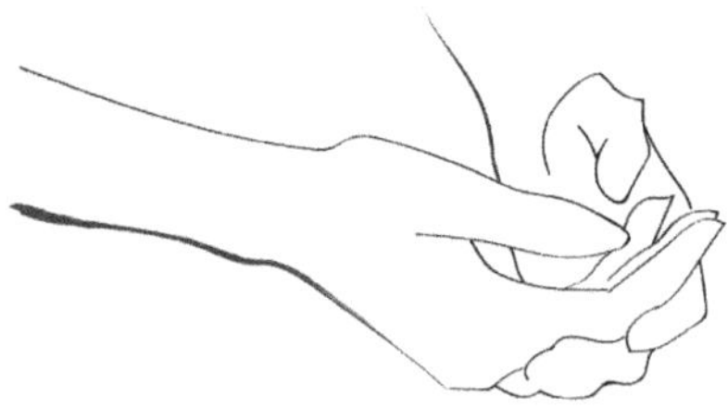

Cement

Build, so I can rent.
I understand what you are saying,
that I should have my own.
I would love that, of course,
but you see,
a home, even if not in your own name,
is better than none.

A home,
where I am warm and safe,
without mould or smashed windows,
is better than none.

Build, so one day I can have a home in my name
too.
It is not mutually exclusive all the time.
Please build,
so I can rent,
and have a home to go to.

Tick tock

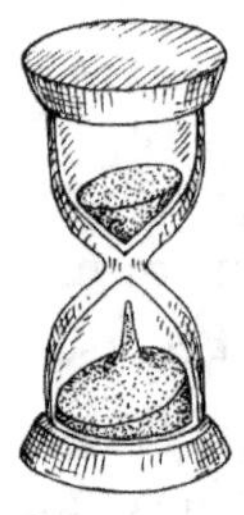

Why did I agree?
When I know there is no time,
my own enemy.

Not again

The heart is a little confused.
The gates were permanently closed,
double locked,
the key thrown away.
Why then can it feel a flutter?

The brain is alarmed.
Not again, not after last time,
the muscles have only just recovered.

A pleasant sight,
a warm smile.
Eyes, you need to avert,
no don't close the eyes,
you'll only propel yourself into an imaginary
world.

A fragment of my own imagination,
neither boon nor destruction,
closed eyes create a different world.

Inconvenient,
but not entirely pointless,
even if fleeting,
it still has a purpose.

Poison

If you can look at a newborn baby,
a baby that cannot hold up their head,
and think they are a threat,
because of their ancestry, their country of birth –

you know what I am going to say,
but I just realised,
you don't actually care.

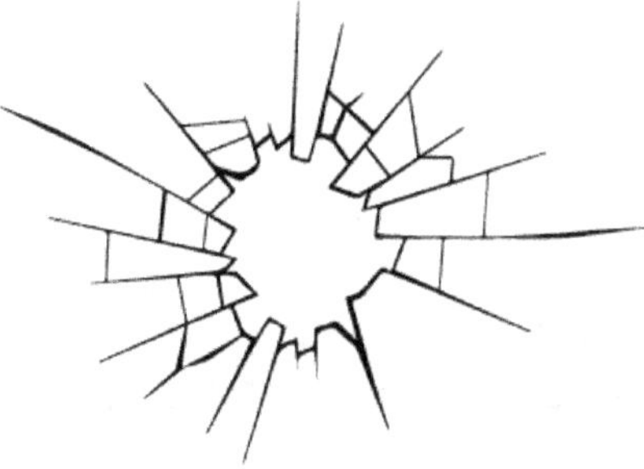

Pebble throwing

They know better than to say,
where are you really from?
Or you are articulate, more competent than they
thought.
Instead, they will ask to see all your workings,
your correspondence, your notes,
they say it is because they want to reassure
themselves that nothing is wrong,
apparently that is ok to say.

They have been told not to tell another to 'smile
more',
they have been advised it is patronising,
as is calling someone brave,
for completing an everyday task,
that they are fully capable of finalising.

Adaptability is the key.
They have found other ways,
to question your abilities,
criticise your inclusion,
throwing pebbles, to wake up your inner critic.

The pebbles will keep coming,
build your wall,
find your tribe, your army,
guard yourself from them.

Travelling to Singapore

When is a holiday, much more than that?
When a princess has to slay the dragon,
just to get to the airport.

The princess, along with her mother,
stuck in an open, iron cage,
free to move within,
unable to open the gates.

Riddled with responsibility,
jumping over mountains,
because of a selfish dragon owner,
forcing the dragon to spit fire,
for no good reason.

The princess is undeterred,
determined to reach the lion city,
she directs her mother to push forward,
break down those gates.

They soar through the skies,
with the aid of a friendly eagle,
waving at the banded surili,
landing at their home away from home.

The princess wins the battle,
and now it is time to sleep.
For she may be the bravest princess of them all,
but she still has a bedtime.

Hadrian's wall

An engineering feat,
73 miles,
the remnants of an empire,
symbolising its might and reach,
defensive.

For me, it is just home.

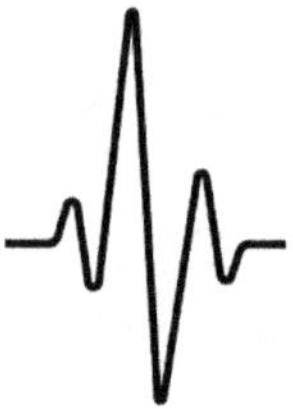

Star-crossed

Postcode lottery,
star-crossed,
coins deciding the meanders.

Vulnerable being taken advantage of,
discriminated,
abused,
perpetrators confident,
of being safe.
Going from door to door,
knocking,
seeking help,
no light at the end of the tunnel.

The scales of justice are intact,
but being able to see them in action,
questionable,
unless, of course,
you possess the power of money.

Surely a sign of a broken system,
a failing society,
where even the rule of law is locked away,

chained,
unable to welcome all.

Sunday night

Sunday night is here.
Uneasiness has arrived with it.
Nausea.
Dread, pinning me down, unable to move.
A constant occurrence, like clockwork.
You know it is on its way.

No amount of preparation can keep it at bay.
Insipid.
Ghosts of the past failures.
Horror stories of when you got it wrong.
The phantom has appeared.

A prayer

Thank you for everything,
without you, I would be nothing.
Please keep me safe,
please keep me sane,
my loved ones,
and humanity too.

Please forgive me my errors,
the times when I forget to seek help,
or show gratitude,
perhaps even to remember.

Please continue to protect us,
shower us with your blessings,
be kind,
to those who have departed already too.

Thank you for everything,
the lessons, as much as the rewards.
Without you, I would be nothing.